The Wedding Officiant's Handbook

A Guide for Wedding Celebrants

Special Section for Ontario Officiants

Bishop Deborah L Vaughan

Gate Street Books

Copyright 2017   Paperback edition

Table of Contents

Introduction

Things change. In the past, only Justices of the Peace, ordained priests and ministers, and those with special permission were permitted to officiate at weddings in Ontario.

More and more, non-religious and wedding-focused organizations are offering certification for those who would like to marry people. Many men and women who have been 'certified' or 'ordained' have asked for my advice or assistance, expressing a need for more training as they assume the duties of a wedding celebrant. Those questions and my own experience form the basis of this little guide.

So, you have your license to marry people – or perhaps you are considering applying to be certified. As we begin, the first question to ask yourself is, "Why am I attracted to this line of work?"

From the outside, being a wedding celebrant seems like a fun and easy way to earn money. Everyone is having a great time, you are part of a very special occasion and, well, you just have to read the script, right? But as many have learned, a wedding celebrant bears a great responsibility and duty.

When you agree to officiate at someone's wedding, you are entering into a legal contract. Fulfilling that contract is more than just reading a ceremony off a paper and remembering to fill in the correct names. It is the beginning of a connection that can last for years.

During the planning process, the couple will look to you to guide them through the myriad of details involved with their ceremony. They may be nervous. They will look to you to be the expert and the trouble-shooter. And, they will expect you to provide them with a meaningful, once-in-a-lifetime experience on the most important day of their lives.

This guide will help prepare you to be a joyful, confident, competent, in-demand celebrant.

You will definitely earn your money, but hopefully, you will find rewards in so many ways that the payment becomes secondary. Being a wedding officiant is like no other work. It can be very challenging. It can make your heart soar. It can draw on resources and gifts you never knew you had. At the heart of it all, this work is all about service, about ministry, about celebrating love in all its fullness.

I have been officiating weddings for 30 years, first as an Anglican priest and now as the presiding bishop for the Community Catholic Church of Canada. I have officiated at everything from religious ceremonies to handfastings, from five-minute civil-type ceremonies to full-blown church weddings with a communion component.

I have been involved in weddings that were absolutely perfect and those that were a comedy of errors – fainting grooms, forgotten rings, vows exchanged in the pouring rain, brides that had second thoughts…. One learns to go with the flow and get very creative when necessary.

I do come at this from a Western, Christian perspective so the history and experience I present comes from that window.

I am also aware that many people reading this material are likely not ordained clergy. For me, marriage is a sacrament, an outward sign of the love that shines forth from within the couple and a connection to Divine Love, Godself.

The wedding is certainly a legal contract with promises and a pronouncement, signed and witnessed and registered with the province, but the marriage and the loving bond that brings people together represents so much more.

Whether you come at this from a religious, spiritual or secular perspective, I know this guide will offer assistance.

As we begin our exploration of the elements of a wedding, let's look at some historical highlights to gain an overview of the marriage covenant.

CHAPTER 1

The Celebration of a Marriage

A Bit of Background

Throughout the centuries, couples of all cultures, traditions and faiths have held ceremonies to make their commitment and love for one another "official" in some way.

The word "wed" comes from an Anglo Saxon word that literally translates to "a man makes vows to marry a certain woman." "Wed" is a word that signifies a contract, so the "wedding" is the occasion where the contract is declared in public. Of course, since the dawn of history, the peoples of the world have called this intentional union of a couple many names and celebrated it in many ways.

Whether it was a public expression of promises, tying ribbons around wrists as a symbol of being eternally connected to one another (ie. "tying the knot"), jumping over a broom together or even drinking out of a common cup, the declaration of a couple's love for one another has long been cause for great celebration and joy.

The history of the customs and traditions of marriage can make for interesting reading and we can still see the remnants of those ancient celebrations in our modern-day ceremonies. Looking into the reasons behind why we do the things a certain way in a ceremony can be very enlightening and bring new understanding.

For example, in the middle ages in Europe and the UK, the custom of having bridesmaids and groomsmen arose from a time in history when the bride was often the subject of a kidnapping.

Some stories explain that this was actually a fun custom. One of the roles of the attendants in the bridal party was to arrange a kidnapping and not allow the groom to see the bride until the wedding. Still there were real occasions of danger and the groomsmen and noble groom would indeed be called upon to defend the bride. So, even today, the groom stands to the bride's right so that his sword hand is free in case of altercation.

Brides were believed to be lucky. The custom of the bride throwing the bouquet was a kind of diversionary tactic to keep the ladies busy so they would not chase after her and tear bits of her dress as talismans. Hence, throwing the bouquet was a strategy for the bride to save herself and the garments she was wearing and make a quick exit to a waiting carriage.

It is also suggested that the wedding bouquet itself, besides being a lovely decorative element, masked body odors of everyone involved since access to bathing facilities was often limited.

As with many customs handed down from generation to generation, the original meaning or intent can get lost along the way. A little research into the meanings and background of things we often take for granted in a ceremony can be really enlightening and provide some fun information to share with your couple.

Notes:

Chapter 2

The Sacrament of Holy Matrimony

Development

It is important for celebrants to understand the historical perspective of marriage – even if you aren't religious -- because the Church has played a major role in shaping the ceremonies that we have today.

Since the days of the Early Church, the Sacrament of Holy Matrimony was viewed as one of the lesser sacraments (along with Penance and Extreme Unction) based on Jesus' first public miracle at the wedding in Cana. But through the first ten centuries, the Church had very little to do with blessing couples at their public declarations.

It is interesting that for those first centuries, marriages were seen as a private affair between a couple without any clergy present - just family and the community. In many cultures, marriage was a rite of passage with the understanding that the couple would take their place in the community, build a life together and have children.

Up to the 19th century, marriages were often arranged by parents, sometimes from the child's birth. At the time of the wedding, the bride could be as young as 12 years of age and she had no say in her parent's choice. The marriage was considered to be a life-long union. Divorce could be obtained by a judge only under extreme conditions.

In the face of the Reformation by the Protestants, The Council of Trent in 1547 set out to reform and more fully organize the Roman Church and define the seven sacraments and set them into Canon Law. During this council the subject of marriage was more clearly defined, pronouncing that couples must now choose each other freely, with parental permission.

It became church law that for the marriage to be holy and recognized by the Church, the couple must make their vows before a priest or bishop and have two witnesses present, otherwise the marriage was not considered valid. Our present day ceremony includes a question that the couple chooses each other freely with no impediment. This requirement stems from that 16th century canon law.

So through that long ago council, marriage became promoted as an important, sacred and sacramental act of expression and intention between a committed couple.

A Promise Given and Received

For us who come at this from a more religious background, this is the heart of the sacrament. While there are prayers, readings, music and elements that can be added in to the ceremony, the thing that makes marriage one of the sacraments, is the covenant, the solemn promises made between the couple.

The priest, the congregation, the liturgy, and the setting are all secondary to these promises. The sacrament is a contract between the couple that is recognized and blessed by God and we are all witnesses to that intention.

So, with the new understanding promoted by the 16th century Council, the marriage vows, freely exchanged, signaled a new beginning in the life of the couple – a mutual decision, not one forced on the bride or the groom by parents. The couple gained a new status in society as they promised a life based on mutual help, support, and comfort through the years.

These were now open-ended vows: "for better or worse, richer or poor, in sickness and in health," expressing an unconditional love that befitted Christian charity and echoing the love Christ has for the Church.

And, included in the expression of this life-long commitment came a promise of fidelity and the expressed intention of building a family together. These vows have been expressed in some form or other since the deliberations of the Trent Council, and still largely shapes our rites and customs today in the Western world.

Notes:

Chapter 3
Where are you in the Picture?

Defining Who You Are As Celebrant

I am aware that many of you reading this guide may have no faith affiliation. It has been suggested that up to 80% of couples looking for an officiant have little or no connection with church or faith community. However, that doesn't mean they aren't looking for a spiritual experience.

They may not want "God-talk" but unless the couple has staunch atheistic views, they are looking for a ceremony that celebrates their love and offers elements that speak to the eternal and forever quality of their connection.

It is important that you determine for yourself where you are comfortable. If a couple comes to you and wants a more religious tone to the wedding, are you comfortable saying prayers, reading Christian scripture and talking about Jesus or the Trinity?

If the couple is interfaith and wants to combine elements of both religions are you okay with that? If the couple is pagan and requests a handfasting, can you do that and also include the necessary requirements for the Ontario government?

I once had a request from a couple to do a wedding in a backyard which isn't an issue - I regularly officiate at people's homes. *This* request was a little different. They were nudists and wanted to get married "au naturel." That prompted some deep thought on my part. I finally decided that if it was their custom and chosen lifestyle I could support that, but I was keeping *my* clothes on, thank you. As it happened, they didn't call back. I am certain that someone else was able to welcome their request more enthusiastically.

I know where my strengths are and I know how best to serve my couples. I don't think shedding my clothes to solemnize a marriage is in my wheelhouse. I am not eager to go up in a helicopter to perform a marriage over Niagara Falls as some of my colleagues in this area do. I am happy to let them help those couples.

We all have growing edges and we are not expected to know everything about every single faith group or culture. But as officiants who will be engaged with a diverse population, it is essential to know where *our* growing edges are and what to do about them.

For more than 20 years, I was largely dealing with parishioners looking to get married in a church. Up until very recently in the Anglican Church, that meant using the prayerbook and holding the ceremony in an approved chapel. It meant taking time with each couple to plan the wedding and then sending them off on a special weekend to offer more intensive preparation for the marriage.

Now that I am no longer in that system and can offer a more couple-centric ceremony, there is a trade off. I find I don't get the chance to know my couples as well as I did before. In dealing with younger brides and grooms especially, there is sometimes an awkwardness about how to relate to me – which usually dissipates after we chat and they discover I like to have fun as much as they do.

It is important to schedule a meeting in person, on Skype or speakerphone and take time to get to know them. Have the couple share some history with you. You will find that some couples are very happy to tell you about their life and relationship. Others you may find are not as forthcoming and that is okay. It isn't a third degree -- the idea is to make a connection and promote a sense of trust and non-judgment.

I always ask conversational questions like: how long have they known each other? How did they meet? What is their favorite thing about each other? Are they living together already? Do they have children? Are there kids from other relationships? In this way I begin to get a picture of how to help create a wonderful ceremony and incorporate elements that are meaningful for the couple and their family.

Sometimes, when speaking to a couple, you'll hear about significant people in their lives who have passed away or are unable to be there. It is important to be an ear for them. In your role as celebrant, you are seen as someone who understands and can offer words of guidance or comfort. You may be the closest thing they have to clergy in their lives, and it is at pivotal life events that questions arise about life and death and the big questions. Be prepared to respond from the heart.

Many celebrants get into the work because officiating at weddings seems like a cut and dry kind of thing. You show up, say the words, and then sign the paperwork. If you do it well, you'll discover that it is so much more. It is an absolute privilege. It can be messy. It is emotional. It involves dealing with people under stressful conditions. It offers the opportunity to meet some wonderful families and share an experience that is life-changing when done well.

Remember, you are not just another vendor – anyone can read the words of a wedding ceremony. As celebrant, *you* bring meaning and blessing to it all.

As you consider the experiences you have had, what worked well for you? Where did you feel you could have done more? What do you want to work on? There is your growing edge.

Notes:

Chapter 4

The Nuts and Bolts of Officiating: Your Wedding Business

Administration

As an independent celebrant, it is important to set up your services as a business. For those of us who have been part of a church system, the idea of hanging out the shingle may be a little daunting, and for many who belong to a wedding company much of the administrative work may be done for you already, but setting up your own company can bring benefits for other offerings you may have.

Getting a master business licence in your name or the name of your business is the first step. In this way, you can set up a business account with your bank and also set up a business account with Paypal, if you choose. This makes it much easier to receive monies for your services.

A website and a facebook page are always a good things. There you can express yourself, post news and build a following. You can introduce yourself and list the services you offer. You can also set up Paypal buttons on your website.

There are many excellent website building platforms out there. It is easy to build a free website and you can get a package including a domain name fairly inexpensively. There are often sales on packages.

Invest in a nice business card and have some with you at all times. You never know when an opportunity may present to introduce yourself.

Promoting Your Services

Few of us have the resources to advertise in newspapers or magazines. One small ad can be about what you'd charge for a wedding. Wedding shows are also expensive for a one-day event, but it may be a worthwhile expenditure to choose a local show to promote your services to prospective couples. You may even consider teaming up with other vendors for events like these, splitting the costs and doing some effective networking.

There are ways to promote yourself without any out-of-pocket expenses. I have found an ad in kijiji, Craig's List or online bulletin boards can generate many responses.

People are searching online and in many cases are looking for simple and inexpensive ways to have a wedding. Couples are shopping around for the right officiant at the most economical price. You can slant your ad to address that need. There are other free sites like Craigslist that can also boost your business.

There are also several wedding-focused websites that have excellent reputations and attract a lot of traffic. WeddingWire is one of the best, in my view, and offers a free webpage for your wedding business where you can connect with other vendors and receive reviews from your couples. There are paid levels too, but even the free site can draw traffic and increase your web presence.

Do not underestimate the value of word of mouth. Start a blog, tell your friends and family, post little updates on Facebook or Twitter or other social media. Remember that it takes time to build your name and reputation, so don't be discouraged if the phone isn't ringing off the hook immediately. There are cycles and seasons in the wedding world and some weeks will be busier than others. I have learned not to worry about how busy other officiants may or may not be and I don't fret if the phone is quiet. What is for you will come to you.

You can find more ways to promote yourself and your business in my e-book "100 Ways to Promote Your Wedding Business."

Creating the Plan

So, you have a website and promotion in place. You have a business license and a pile of cards. Now, you need to consider how to operate your business most effectively.

For some people this will be pre-determined by the company you work with, but if not, think about how much you wish your honorarium to be for a wedding and how far you are willing to travel.

Think about hosting weddings in your home if space allows. Many people are looking for simple places where they can be married, then have a big party elsewhere to celebrate. Perhaps you can accommodate them in a backyard gazebo or cozy space by the fireplace.

Pricing

There is no question that weddings can be expensive for couples. The rates for officiants vary widely, but remember, couples are paying for your time and your expertise. Do not be shy to ask for monies that will cover your time, travel and the preparation spent with the couple.

It is always a little interesting to me that a fabulous amount of money can been invested in a dress, flowers, cake, music and the reception, yet because we are clergy, some people think our services should be inexpensive. Without the ceremony, there would be no cause for the rest of the celebration!

You know, as officiants you are providing a legal service including the filing of paperwork. What do lawyers and paralegals charge for three hours of their labour?

When considering your services, it is important that you honour yourself. See what other officiants are charging in your area and offer a competitive price.

It is also important to recognize that there are a lot of other officiants out there and more arriving on the scene all the time. I know at times that my fee has been undercut by other officiants who are more assertive than I at getting clients.

My philosophy is that there is enough for all. I know someone who does upwards of 800 weddings in a year and steps on many toes to do it. That is not my goal. I truly believe that the couples who come to me are meant for me.

I see this as ministry and that is my focus. I believe that I would not be able to have the quality connections that I enjoy if I had more than three weddings every day. It is important for you to think about a comfortable number of weddings for you to book.

We have addressed getting a website, using social media, considering your market and determining what your fees may be. You've considered the kinds of weddings you'd like to perform, growing edges and comfort levels. Let's now turn our attention to the process of the booking a ceremony.

Notes:

Chapter 5
Step By Step Wedding Planning

When a couple approaches you to do their wedding, there are important steps to take to ensure you have the data you will need.

Booking Your Services

A Deposit Is a Must

Once it as been ascertained that the date and time for a couple's wedding are available, it is a very good idea to request a deposit of at least $100 to confirm the wedding. Upon receipt of the deposit, you may wish to make a formal confirmation letter detailing your responsibilities and including the balance owing. Some will pay the entire fee at once and a confirmation email or letter outlining that should be sent.

The deposit should be non-refundable. In early days it sometimes happened that I received the deposit, took time to assist with ideas and plans, only to learn that they decided to book elsewhere or postpone the wedding for various reasons. There was often an expectation that the deposit monies would be returned and my time and effort were offered without thanks or compensation. The deposit is the recognition of the time taken and honours your expertise.

Accepting Payments

On the subject of payment, think about the ways in which you would like to receive monies. The deposit is non-refundable, but when and how would you like to receive the balance?

Many officiants ask for cash on the day, if the balance hasn't been received before the wedding. It has happened that over the years that last-minute cheque has bounced at the bank, then it becomes a matter of chasing and invoicing after the fact, when the event has been enjoyed and often the money has been spent. It is important to be very clear and business-like.

You can always hold their wedding license until payment is received as some do, but it is best to avoid this altogether and ensure the wedding is paid in full prior to the date. Other wedding vendors are spelling out their terms, and we should too.

Paypal business accounts are easily set up to allow for online payments. Email money transfers are becoming more and more popular as a method of payment. You may wish to talk to your bank or financial institution about setting up a Point of Sales terminal for your business. That way you can accept credit cards and debit cards and offer another convenient way for your couples to pay you.

There are many convenient platforms such as Square, which is portable and very easy to manage.

The Data You Need

When you have received the deposit and have confirmed the wedding with the couple you will need all their information. You may wish to send along the basic ceremony as an attachment with the confirmation of your services.

The following is a form that I have created to assist with everything I need at a glance.

I have a binder specifically for weddings, divided by month with about 25 blank forms ready to go. Once I book a wedding, the form goes into the appropriate month and is also entered into my day timer.

Sample Information Form
Parish Letterhead

Date of call:
Have either been divorced outside of Canada?

Payment - Cost of your Clergy Services based on basic fee plus any extras
Balance - how much was received and how, how much is left to pay
Method of Payment

Full names of the couple
Info: address(es), phone numbers, cell phone, email

Wedding Details:
- Time, Date, Venue
- What kind of ceremony are they looking for?

Elopement, civil (like justice of the peace, short and simple), spiritual,   religious, religious with Mass?

- How many people are in the wedding party? Flower girl? Ring Bearer? Is the Bride being escorted?
- Will they want a rehearsal? (extra charge for this)
- If elopement, will they need witnesses (extra charge for this)
- Are they looking to include a special element? Sand ceremony? Rose Ceremony? Wine Box?
- Will there be special music? (Often the couple will hire musicians. Sometimes, they send music for me to play on my iPad.)
- Any special things to note in the ceremony? Sometimes couples want to remember those who cannot be a part of the celebration and may light a candle in their memory)
 - space for notes

See Appendix at the back of this booklet for a template you can use

Notes:

Chapter 6

The Process of Planning the Wedding

Consultation:

Sometimes the couple will want to meet you in person rather than discuss details over the phone or via email. As often as possible, invite them to meet at your office, home or nearby coffee shop to save you travel and gas expenditures. Some couples will have a few exchanges and feel comfortable, others may lean a little harder and require more attention. Each wedding is different and as you get to know your couple, you'll have a sense of how best to assist them, and how much time you are willing to offer for your price point.

Planning the wedding day details with your couple:

When talking to your couple, go over the flow of the wedding. If they are holding the wedding at a hotel or hall, there is often a coordinator appointed for the day. This helps the organization and flow of the ceremony greatly. The onsite coordinator will line up the bridal party and make sure that everything is going to schedule.

Here is an outline of the order of most weddings and a timeline to discuss with the couple. They may have a coordinator who will be responsible for all this, but this is the general order of things FYI.

- 45 minutes before the wedding the ushers (if any) should be on site to seat guests

- 30 minutes before, you arrive and will need the licence

- 15 minutes before the ceremony, the groom should be present in the venue with his groomsmen. Same applies to same-sex couples, unless they are walking in together.

- 5 minutes before the ceremony, groom's party should be up at the front with you. The groom stands to your left and groom's men line up starting with the nest man, closest to groom. Have the groom stand facing you till the bride enters the room. Groomsmen can stand a little in profile so they can look at the congregation.

At this point, the wedding is about to begin.

Traditional Line Up

Groom's Side	Bride + Escort Maid/matron of Honour Bridesmaids Flower Girl and Ringbearer Groomsmen, Best Man, **GROOM** (Bridal party will be here) Officiant	Bride's Side

Groom's parents are seated.

Bride's mom (or special person) is seated. (Sometimes the groomsmen will escort them in and then take their place up front) There may be special music for this.

The bridal party line- up:
  Flower girl/ring bearer,
  Bridesmaids,
  Maid/Matron of honour,
  Bride and escort (if any).

- Note that sometimes the flower girl and ring bearer *may* go immediately in front of the bride. They do tend to take attention away from the bride in this position, because they are so darn cute.

Bridesmaids will enter and go to your right, lining up to match the groomsmen. It is helpful to have a game plan for the flower girl and ring bearer, as they are often young and need an adult to hold onto them.

Sometimes there is special music for the entrance of the first part of the wedding party and then a different tune to signal the entrance of the Bride.

The bride enters with or without escort and joins the groom.

The ceremony takes place. (Outline will be discussed in the next section.)

The licence and register are signed at the **end** of the ceremony. (It is important that you familiarize yourself with the legal requirements of the jurisdiction you are in. Every State, County and Province has its own set of protocol and rules. Ensure that you can direct your couple and fill out the paperwork with confidence.)

The couple is announced, signaling the end of the wedding.

Music is generally played.

The Recession goes as follows:
- Bride and groom leave first
- Best Man and Maid/Matron of Honour
- flower girl and ring bearer, if they are still there
- one bridesmaid and one groomsmen meet up and leave
  together until done

Planning and follow-up Consultations before the wedding

You may be called on to meet or speak with the couple on a few occasions. Once they have selected options in the ceremony, then a subsequent email can be sent to clarify your role for the wedding.

Let them know when you will arrive and remind them that you will need the marriage licence upon arrival. Also, make sure they know there must be a table set up for the signing of the paperwork. If they are getting married in a non-professional venue like a backyard garden, this is often a detail that is overlooked.

Rehearsals

In my experience, rehearsals are largely unnecessary. By the time the wedding arrives, I will have spoken with the couple on several occasions and discussed the choreography of the day. (How will they process in, where are they standing at the venue, how will they leave, etc.)

Unless the bride is very nervous or the wedding is complicated, a rehearsal is not usually needed. There is an extra charge for a rehearsal because for us, a rehearsal is like doing the wedding. It takes time and often, travel and gas. Most officiants charge $100 for a rehearsal.

Notes for You for The Wedding Day

What to Wear?

Unless it is specifically requested otherwise, I always wear a clergy collar. For those of you who are not ordained, this won't be an option, of course.

Over the past few years, I have moved from wearing a contemporary kind of robe to a simple business suit. This is often because weddings can take place in blazing sunlight in screaming summer temps and it is just too hot to wear so many layers of clothing.

Most couples are not religious, so wearing a cassock or robe seems out of place. But there are some interesting styles of robes available that would be most appropriate and festive should you choose to vest for a wedding.

If you are not clergy, you have several options. Some officiants wear a business suit or dress. Others wear a choir robe. Some choose formal wear. Whatever you choose, it should be comfortable, look professional and fit well. You will be in thousands of photos over the years.

Arrival

It is a good thing to be onsite about 30 minutes prior to the wedding if possible. In this way you can meet with coordinators, photographer, musicians, and guests. Also, you can ensure that the area is set up to your satisfaction. If elements such as a unity candle or sand ceremony are included, double check that all the material is present and set up on a table.

Ask for the licence upon arrival. If there are things to fill in before the ceremony, you can take time to do that first thing. **Note:** If there is a problem and the license is not available, you may have to alter the ceremony, making it a commitment ceremony without any legal references to marriage, husband, wife and you will not pronounce them. It happens from time to time that the license has not been arranged or sometimes is misplaced. This happened to me recently, when some well meaning friends packing up the couples' room tossed it in the trash without realizing its importance. (The hotel staff did know and saved the day.) You cannot do a marriage ceremony without the license, but you can do a non-legal alternative that will sound like a wedding.

If there is any balance owing, ask for it upon arrival. It is a good policy to have the couple clear up the balance before the wedding day, saving you this step. Often in the busyness of the day, cheques can be left at home or forgotten. Consider offering a small discount for balances paid 48 hours before the wedding to encourage timely payments.

Have an officiant care pack with you: a bottle of water, tissues, breath mints, headache reliever and several pens. I have found that a 9x7 zippered leather binder with pockets makes an excellent ceremony book.

As the time to begin approaches, you may have to hustle the wedding party a little and keep time. If the bride is a little late, it isn't usually a problem. If the bride is very late or the wedding is delayed it could mean that your next appointment is in jeopardy.

Getting stuck in traffic is one thing, but a bride sipping tea and still looking at her wedding dress 5 minutes before you are set to begin is being intentionally draggy. Not good for your blood pressure. A time fine is a good deterrent. Knowing they have to pay an additonal charge is effective.

There is a certain clergyperson in this area who simply leaves if the couple isn't ready within 10 minutes of the start time. He also leaves if they haven't got a balance cheque. That is the way he chooses to handle things. It may not be your way. You have to decide how you will deal with these issues. Sometimes things start late because the couple is disorganized but sometimes things just cannot be helped. It is up to your own judgment how best to handle late starts.

After the wedding, make sure the couple receives their part of the wedding licence, if applicable.

Following the wedding, you may wish to make up a form letter of sorts congratulating and thanking the couple. Remind them that it can take up to 12 weeks to process their licence and all the information they need is in the forms they received when they got the licence. Voila!

Notes:

Chapter 7
Creating the Ceremony

If you have surfed online looking at all the various ceremonies and options offered out there, you can get very confused. Some ceremonies are frankly horrible and very poorly written, including elaborate elements that make a spectacle rather than a simple liturgy that has at the heart of it the loving intention and promises of the couple.

As representatives of the province, we have to ascertain that the couple is there of their own free will and there are no impediments to the union.

We also have to ensure that there are at least two witnesses on hand. In the province of Ontario there is no age restriction for witnesses. A child who can write their name may sign paperwork at the discretion of the parents and celebrant. If they understand what is happening then they may witness and sign.

There is no need to see ID or passports etc. By the time the couple is granted a licence from the wedding office any legal impediment has been cleared, so it follows that there really isn't a concern unless someone is having second thoughts.

As officiants, we will find that we have couples from all faiths and walks of life, along with those who identify as Christian. I seldom do a full out religious ceremony unless a gay or lesbian couple who would not otherwise have opportunity to celebrate their marriage in their church requests it.

It is important then to have several options to offer couples. It may be that you are part of a church or organization that has a standard ceremony and that is okay, but for those who are looking for direction on the elements of a wedding ceremony, the next section will be of interest.

The Form of the Marriage Ceremony

There is a natural flow to the wedding ceremony. Above all, it is a celebration of the couple and their intention to build a life together in a committed and legal relationship.

Most of the couples who approach us to officiate may have roots in a church but no longer attend. Most of the weddings we do will take place in venues other than a church or chapel. As officiants, we bring the authority of the government with us as we celebrate weddings.

Once the bride and groom are standing in front of us, it is our responsibility to set the tone and pace of the liturgy. They will be nervous and will be relying on us to get them through it, having a good time in the process. So, be light of heart and catch their excitement and that will connect you all as you begin.

There are set parts of the ceremony that follow a certain order. They are as follows:

* Procession (usually to music)
* Welcome and Introductory Words about marriage (This can include the question,
   "Who gives this woman in marriage" but very often this is not requested any more)
* Readings (optional)
   Note: Special Music can be played after reading(s) if there

is a soloist, etc.

* Declarations (Asking the bride and groom if they choose to marry each other)
* Questions of Support from the congregation (optional)
* The Vows
* The Exchange of Rings
* Optional Elements (Unity Candle, Sand Ceremony, Flower Ceremony, Love

   Letter Ceremony etc. More about these in another section.)
* Blessing of the Couple
* Pronouncement and The Kiss
* Signing of the Register (sometimes special music is played here too)
* Announcement of the Couple (I present N&N, married couple or Mr & Mrs X, if they choose... always ask ahead of time how they would like to be announced.)
* Recessional

This order follows the traditional outline based on church liturgies and it just works. I have participated in ceremonies that put the unity candle at the end after the kiss and it just seemed to interrupt the flow. The kiss is the signal that were done except for the paperwork. :)

Notes:

Chapter 8
Unpacking it All

Ideally, the ceremony should be between 20 to 30 minutes in length. Elopements are usually about 15 minutes long because couples want something more simple at this kind of ceremony.

Ceremony Template

The Entrance/Processional

* Teaching point to share with the couple*
As the bride arrives at the front with escort (often dad), coach the groom to step forward. The escort will shake groom's hand, kiss bride and place her hand in his, then take his/her place beside bride's mom/special person.

As the couple stands in front of you, the groom will be to your left and the bride to your right. Have them join a hand and turn and face each other a little. This allows the congregation to see and hear them and is better for photos.

The Introduction:

This part of the ceremony sets the tone of the gathering. It states the reason for the gathering, a bit about the couple's journey together, words about marriage and what is about to happen and ends with a prayer or an affirmation for the couple.

Readings
There are many wonderful readings that can be used to add a layer of meaning to the proceedings. Some prefer to have a

biblical reading, often asking for 1 Cor 13. Others have used song lyrics or meaningful passages from other inspired writers. Because this is a wedding that expresses the promises of the couple and their "personality." I often let them set the tone on this.

Members of the family or friends can offer the reading (s).

The Declarations

As we begin the contractual part of the ceremony, the declarations are questions posed to each of the couple with specific references to their intentions. "Do you promise?" In other words, these questions show that the couple is there of their own free will and are ready and willing to make promises to each other.

Assuming they answer in the affirmative, they are ready to say their vows.

The Vows

At this point, direct the bride to hand her flowers to the M of Honour. Have them turn and face each other and join both hands. Remind them to repeat after you in a loud voice.

The vows are the centrepiece of the wedding. Even though there may be a costly huge reception and party to come, this is the real reason why everyone has assembled. There are many wonderful vows that can be offered as options besides the traditional vows that everyone knows. I encourage couples to write their own promises to each other. This can be very powerful.

It is also important to remember that the couple will be nervous and longer vows can seem like hours to say. I have one vow option that is very long and couples routinely select it because it is beautiful. Longer vows can add time to the ceremony and can also be a lot for couples to repeat. Speak to them about this when you are planning the ceremony. Some just want short and sweet.

Sometimes couples wish to say different vows to each other. This is not a problem. Some couples will want to repeat after you, others will want to read from a paper. There is no right or wrong way. However, for personal vows it is always best if they say them directly to each other.

The Ring Ceremony

Most couples will each exchange a ring these days. Early in my ministry, it wasn't uncommon for just the bride to receive a ring, but now, double rings are the norm.

Even those who are not really religious love the ritual of the blessing and so it is a nice thing to talk about the symbol of the ring and what it means before they exchange it. Just by our nature we are blessing the rings with our words and intentions, but often the couple will ask for a special blessing on them.

* Teaching point to share with the couple*
As the rings are exchanged, here is a teaching point for the couple that I call "the ring flip." As the groom takes the bride's left hand in his and puts on the ring, have them continue to hold onto each other's hand and just flip it so that the bride is now holding the groom's left hand. You'd be surprised how many couples forget which is the left hand.

In this way, they are all ready to continue as she says her words. Remind them quietly, "Hold and flip!" They always smile.

There are many things that can be said as the rings are exchanged and the vows are sealed.

Other Elements

Adding these elements to the ceremony means that you and the couple must move to a table or another place in the venue. Direct the couple to follow you and position them so that they will be in the best location for photos.

After you are finished, invite them to follow you back and take their place once more.

There are several beautiful elements that can be added to the ceremony to highlight the symbolic union of two souls in marriage.

Some of these include:
A Unity Candle (the bride and groom light the one centre candle with two tapers. A nice touch is when the mothers, who gave them life, offer them the lit candles so the couple can in turn light the one centre candle together.)

A Sand Ceremony (two colours of sand are poured into a centre container, making a unique pattern that reflects the union of the couple.

Note: This is also a wonderful activity for blended families. Everyone gets a colour of sand and they all take turns pouring sand into the one container. It is a beautiful visual representation of the special day when they became one family together.)

A Love Letter Ceremony (A Swedish tradition that has the bride and groom writing each other private love letters, sealing them in envelopes. The couple select two bottles of wine or something they like to drink and get a box that can be locked or sealed in some way. If down the road they run into trouble, they get the box, take out the letters, go into different rooms and read them, then come back, drink the wine and talk things out.)

There are variations on this. I tend to encourage having the bridal party back in a few years to have a reading of the letters, a toast with the wine and perhaps placing new letters in the box with more wine.

Flower Ceremony (The bride and groom exchange red roses accompanied by beautiful words.
Note - This is a great one to include family members or children. After the bride and groom exchange roses, they then call children forward and give each child a flower, telling them that they will always love them. The flowers are all placed in a vase, a symbol of the new family.)

Other elements can be included here as well.

We continue with…
The Blessing

Time for the bride to receive her flowers once more.
There is much scope for you to wrap up the ceremony. Sometimes I will use the Benediction of the Apaches, sometimes I will use the Blessing of the Hands then say a little blessing to affirm them in their new life together.

The Pronouncement

We've come to the conclusion of the main ceremony. Here we simply review what has taken place and pronounce the couple husband and wife (or husband and husband, or wife and wife or lifepartners... or whatever feels most comfortable). At the invitation for the Kiss, I usually move out of the camera range.

Once they have kissed and everyone has applauded, you will notice a difference in the energy. Tension is gone! And we head to the table to sign the paperwork. Witnesses come too.

The Announcement
Generally, it works best if you take the couple back to the centre once more. That way, leaving the area will flow as the wedding party just reverses the order of entry.

Announce the couple, "It is my privilege and pleasure to introduce to you for the very first time ...." Cheers, applause, often bubbles. Cue the music and invite the bride and groom to hold hands and leave, followed by Best People, followed by first groomsman and first bridesmaid who meet lock arms and head out etc.

Notes:

Appendix One: Wedding Resources - Readings

A quick search for wedding ceremonies will bring up dozens of choices for ceremonies. Some are very formal and others are more relaxed. Some are very poorly written. As you gain experience, you will find ceremonies that work for you the best. As time goes on you will gather wonderful resources for your couples that will serve them as they plan their wedding ceremony with you. Here are a few to get you started.

Reading Resources:

1Corinthians 13 (short version)
A reading from the letter of Paul to the Corinthians
Love is patient, love is kind. It does not envy, it does not boast, it is not proud. It is not rude, it is not self-seeking, it is not easily angered, it keeps no record of wrongs. Love does not delight in evil, but rejoices with the truth. It always protects, always trusts, always hopes, always perseveres.

I carry your heart with me e.e. cummings
i carry your heart with me(i carry it in
my heart) i am never without it(anywhere
i go you go, my dear; and whatever is done
by only me is your doing, my darling)
i fear

no fate(for you are my fate, my sweet) i want
no world(for beautiful you are my world, my true)
and it's you are whatever a moon has always meant
and whatever a sun will always sing is you

here is the deepest secret nobody knows
(here is the root of the root and the bud of the bud
and the sky of the sky of a tree called life; which grows
higher than the soul can hope or mind can hide)
and this is the wonder that's keeping the stars apart

i carry your heart(i carry it in my heart)

On Love by Thomas a Kempis

Love is a mighty power, a great and complete good. Love
alone lightens every burden, and makes rough places smooth.
It bears every hardship as though it were nothing, and renders
all bitterness sweet and acceptable.

Nothing is sweeter than love, nothing stronger, nothing
higher, nothing wider, nothing more pleasant, nothing fuller
or better in heaven or earth; for love is born of God. Love
flies, runs and leaps for joy. It is free and unrestrained.

 Love knows no limits, but ardently transcends all bounds.
Love feels no burden, takes no account of toil, attempts things
beyond its strength. Love sees nothing as impossible, for it
feels able to achieve all things.

It is strange and effective, while those who lack love faint and
fail. Love is not fickle and sentimental, nor is it intent on
vanities. Like a living flame and a burning torch, it surges
upward and surely surmounts every obstacle.

On Marriage- Kahlil Gibran

But let there be spaces in your togetherness, and let the winds
of the heavens dance between you. Love one another, but

make not a bond of love: let it rather be a moving sea between the shores of your souls.

Fill each other's cup but drink not from one cup. Give one another of your bread but eat not from the same loaf. Sing and dance together and be joyous, but let each one of you be alone, even as the strings of the lute are alone though they quiver with the same music. Give your hearts, but not into each other's keeping.

For only the land of Life can contain your hearts. And stand together, yet not too near together, for the pillars of the temple stand apart, and the oak tree and the cypress grow not in each other's shadow.

Readings that work nicely after the ring ceremony:

If a family member or friend reads this, it can be especially touching.

Blessing of the Hands

These are the hands of your best friend, young and strong and full of love for you, that are holding yours on your wedding day, as you promise to love each other today, tomorrow, and forever.

These are the hands that will work alongside yours, as together you build your future. These are the hands that will passionately love you and cherish you through the years, and with the slightest touch, will comfort you like no other.

These are the hands that will hold you when fear or grief fills your mind. These are the hands that will countless times wipe the tears from your eyes; tears of sorrow, and tears of joy. These are the hands that will tenderly hold your children.

These are the hands that will help you to hold your family as one. These are the hands that will give you strength when you need it. And lastly, these are the hands that even when wrinkled and aged, will still be reaching for yours, still giving you the same unspoken tenderness with just a touch.

The following reading works as a stand alone reading at the beginning, but I use it a lot as a concluding blessing when the couple may not appreciate a more Christian blessing.

Benediction of the Apaches

Now you will feel no rain,
For each of you will be shelter to the other.
Now you will feel no cold,
For each of you will be warmth to the other.
Now there is no more loneliness for you.
For each of you will be companion to the other.
Now you are two bodies,
But there is only one Life before you.
Go now to your dwelling place,
To enter into the days of your togetherness.
And may your days be good and long upon the earth.

Appendix Two: Ceremonies

Please note that these ceremonies are my own composition and are under my copyright. You may use them because you have purchased this book. Please do not share this material with other officiants – instead, refer them to this book for purchase.

This is the ceremony I use the most. It suits couples of all spiritualities and circumstances.

A Celebration of Love – All purpose wedding ceremony

Today we gather together with *N & N* to celebrate this transformational moment in their lives as they join hearts and hands in love to become one, together in marriage.

Your separate journeys have brought you to this intersecting place in time, a place of great happiness and fulfillment. You have found your heart's desire in one another. You have discovered that one person within whom you recognize love most completely. It is that beautiful connection that we honour today as you come to be married.

The marriage covenant is a mystical exchange of promise and intention that offers you both continued joy, affirmation, respect and support for the rest of your lives.

The promises you make today, these cherished words that speak of the deep and abiding love that you share, will see you through every storm and celebration to come.

Today *N & N* , by joining hands, exchanging vows and rings and expressing your intention to build a future together, your lives are transformed and now merge into one.

May the love that has called you together grow ever brighter and more brilliant with each sunrise, and may these vows offered today bring you joy and great delight in one another for all the days to come.

(If readings are to be incorporated, they are included here.)

The Declarations

N, will you take N to be your wife/lifepartner? Will you stand by her/him no matter what happens, respecting her/him as a person, understanding her/his needs and enjoying her/his love for the rest of your life?

N: I will.

N, will you take N to be your husband/lifepartner? Will you stand by her/him no matter what happens, respecting her/him as a person, understanding her/his needs and enjoying her/his love for the rest of your life?   **N**: I will.

The Vows *(The couple face each other and repeat after Deborah)*

Option 1

N: From this moment, I, N, take you N as my best friend for life. I promise to be your faithful partner and give you my unconditional love. I pledge to honour, encourage and support you through our walk together. I promise to work at our love and always make you a priority in my life. With every beat of my heart I will love you. This is my solemn vow.

Option 2

N: From this day forward, I, N, take you *N* as my best friend for life, the one I will live with, dream with, and love forever. I look with joy down the path of our tomorrows, knowing we will walk it together side by side, hand in hand, and heart to heart. Before us lies an open road, filled with adventure and love. I choose to spend today, and all of my tomorrows, with you as my friend, my wife/husband and my love. This is my solemn vow.

Option 3 - Traditional

I, N, take you, N, to be my wife/husband/lifepartner/spouse
To have and to hold from this day forward;
for better, for worse, for richer, for poorer,
in sickness and in health, to love and to cherish
for the rest of our lives.
This is my solemn vow.

Option 4

N: I, N, take you N, to be my wife/husband/lifepartner/spouse
To laugh with you in joy
To grieve with you in sorrow
To grow with you in love,
To be faithful to you alone for as long as we both shall live.
This is my vow to you.

Option 5

N: I, N, take you N, to be no other than yourself- loving what I know of you, trusting what I do not yet know, with respect for your integrity, and faith in your love for me, through all our years, and in all that life may bring us.

I promise to try to be ever open to you, and to do everything in my power to support you in becoming the person you are yet to be. I promise to love you, to respect you, to laugh with you and to soothe your tears.

I promise to share my life openly and honestly with you; to bring to you the best in me, and to dedicate my time and my energy to you, and to the unfolding of who we are becoming.

I promise to place our relationship at the heart of my life, and not to let the flurry of the everyday eclipse our sacred commitment to one another. This is my solemn vow.

Option 6 – Your own vows

Ring Ceremony

(The rings are given to the Officiant. The couple joins left hands and repeat after the Officiant)

These rings given and received are tokens of the covenant made this day between N & N. Just as the circle of the ring has no beginning and no end, so too their love is unending. Just as the metal is pure and strong, so too the bond between them is certain and steadfast. Let these rings say to all that your commitment is deep and life-long.

N: N, this ring is a token of my faithfulness and love, and a symbol that all I have I share with you.

N: N, this ring is a token of my faithfulness and love, and a symbol that all I have I share with you.

(If additional elements are to be included, they usually are included here.)

The Blessing

As you are joined together in these sacred vows as partners for life, remember that your bond together is upheld and supported at all times by Love in whom we live and move and have our being.

Option 1

May your love together be a true expression of healing and grace. May you always know joy and delight in each other and a deepening of your connection that grows more beautiful every day. May you know with every sunrise and sunset the richness of the love you are called to share.

May you be blessed in your work and in your companionship, in your sleeping and in your waking, in the good times and in the challenges and may harmony, serenity and blessing be the hallmark of your life together.

Option 2

Now you will feel no rain for each of you will be shelter for the other. Now you will feel no cold for each of you will be warmth for the other. Now there is no loneliness for you, because though you are two persons there is only one life before you. As you now enter your life as married partners, may your days together be happy and long.

Pronouncement

N & N, you have declared your love for each other and your hopes for the future. You have made a solemn covenant with each other and have symbolized it by joining hands, by declaring your vows, and by exchanging rings. I now pronounce that you are now husband and wife/ lifepartners.

May your love continue to unite you so that you may be faithful to the vows that you have made this day, and may you live together in joy and peace till your lives end.

You may kiss the bride./You may seal your vows with a kiss.

Signing of the Register

Announce the Couple

Recessional

Copyright 2017 Bishop Deborah Vaughan
http://www.holyangelscommunity.com/
Used with permission

A Celebration of Love
Christian/Catholic Religious Version

Today we come together with N and N to celebrate this transformational moment in their lives as they express their intention to join hearts and hands to become one in the holy sacrament of marriage.

You have each walked a sacred path and by the grace of God you have been brought you to this intersecting place in time, a place of great happiness and fulfillment.

You have found your heart's desire in one another. You have discovered that one person within whom you recognize love most completely. You have come to understand the mystical paradox of the love you share: its deep, strong roots hold you together in a timeless embrace, yet its many strong branches give each of you space to grow and be the wonderful person you are. It is that beautiful connection that we honor today as you come to be married.

As we gather in the loving presence of the Holy Spirit we give thanks for the gift that is love in all its fullness. Together, as one family in Christ, we begin this celebration.

May the grace of our Lord, Jesus Christ and the love of God and the fellowship of the Holy Spirit be with you all.

All: And also with you.

Let us pray:
Gracious God, you have made the bond of marriage a holy mystery, a symbol of Christ' love. Hear our prayer for **N and N**. With faith in you, and each other, they pledge their love

today. May their lives always bear witness to the reality of that love. We ask this through our Lord Jesus Christ, your Son, who lives and reigns with you and the Holy Spirit, one God forever and ever. **Amen.**

A reading from the letter of Paul to the Corinthians

Love is patient, love is kind. It does not envy, it does not boast, it is not proud. It is not rude, it is not self-seeking, it is not easily angered, it keeps no record of wrongs. Love does not delight in evil, but rejoices with the truth. It always protects, always trusts, always hopes, always perseveres.

The Marriage Covenant

N and N, through the Holy Spirit, Christ is present among us and abundantly blesses your love.
As you take hands and offer to one another the vows of the marriage covenant, your lives will be profoundly linked in a new way

The promises you make within this covenant need constant, daily nurturing and attention. By joining hands, exchanging vows and rings and expressing your intention to build a future together, your lives are transformed and now merge into one.

The Declarations

N will you take N to be your husband/wife? Will you stand by him/her no matter what happens, respecting him/her as a person, understanding his/her needs and enjoying his/her love until death parts you? **N: I will.**

N will you take N to be your husband/wife? Will you stand by him/her no matter what happens, respecting him/her as a person, understanding his/her needs and enjoying his/her love until death parts you? **N: I will.**

N and N Since it is your intention to enter into marriage, join your right hands, and declare your consent before God. *(Please look at each other and repeat after me):*

The Vows –
(The couple faces each other and repeats)

Option 1
N: From this moment, I, **N**, take you **N** as my husband/wife/lifepartner. I promise to love, honour, encourage, and support you through our life together. I promise to stand by you and uplift you both in mind and spirit, so that through our union, we can accomplish more than we would alone. This is my vow to you.

Option 2
N: From this day forward, I, N, take you *N* as my best friend for life, the one I will live with, dream with, and love forever. I look with joy down the path of our tomorrows, knowing we will walk it together side by side, hand in hand, and heart to heart. Before us lies an open road, filled with adventure and love. I choose to spend today, and all of my tomorrows, with you as my friend and my love. This is my solemn vow.

Option 3 - Traditional Vows:
I N, take you N, to be my husband/wife/lifepartner
To have and to hold from this day forward;
for better, for worse, for richer, for poorer,
in sickness and in health, to love and to cherish
for the rest of our lives, according to God's Holy Law.
This is my solemn vow.

Option 4 - Your own vows

Ring Ceremony

(The rings are given to the Officiant. The couple joins left hands and repeat after the Officiant)

These rings given and received are tokens of the covenant made this day between N and N. Just as the circle of the ring has no beginning and no end, so too their love is unending. Just as the metal is pure and strong, so too the bond between them is certain and steadfast. Let these rings say to all that your commitment is deep and life-long.

Loving God, bless + these rings given and received that they would be a sign and symbol to all of the deep love that shines forth from within.

N: N, this ring is a token of my faithfulness and love, and a symbol that all I have I share with you in the name of the Father, and of the Son and of the Holy Spirit.

N: N, this ring is a token of my faithfulness and love, and a symbol that all I have I share with you in the name of the Father, and of the Son and of the Holy Spirit.

N and N in love, you have pledged to make your connection flourish, emotionally and spiritually. May that love be a blessing to you both and an inspiration to all those you meet throughout your lives.

The Blessing

As you are joined together in these sacred vows as partners for life, remember that your bond together is upheld and supported at all times by God in whom we live and move and have our being.

May your love together be a true expression of healing and grace in this broken world. May you always know joy and delight in each other and a deepening of your connection that grows more beautiful every day. May you know with every sunrise and sunset the richness of the love you are called to share.

May you be blessed in your work and in your companionship, in your sleeping and in your waking, in your joy and in your challenges. May you be given all that you need to live out with joy the vows and the promises made this day and may harmony, serenity and blessing be the hallmark of your life together.

Pronouncement

N and **N**, you have chosen each other in love and freedom. You have declared your promises before God and those here gathered and you have offered sacred vows to one another. I now pronounce that you are now husband and wife/ lifepartners.

What God has joined together, human beings must not divide.

You may kiss each other.

Signing of the Register
Announce the Couple
Recessional

Copyright 2017 Bishop Deborah Vaughan
http://www.holyangelscommunity.com/
Used with permission

Commitment Ceremony

Sometimes it happens that a couple cannot get married legally but still want to make a public declaration of their loving commitment. Sometimes it has happened that there is a hold up with divorce papers. Sometimes it is a gay or lesbian couple whose marriage wouldn't be recognized back home. Sometimes the couple just don't want legal papers, just a heart to heart commitment.

You must be very careful when performing a commitment ceremony. Because of the authority granted to officiants if we pronounce the couple husband and wife, etc., it is a BINDING agreement. When we pronounce, they are actually married, which can be a problem if they still have divorce materials being processed.

So a commitment ceremony must NOT have vows, but promises. We cannot say anything more than we recognize their love and commitment to one another.

Celebration of Love- Commitment Ceremony

Today we gather together with N & N to witness this transformational moment in their lives as they join hearts and hands to become one in love forever.

You have found your heart's desire in one another. You have discovered that one person within whom you recognize love most completely. It is that beautiful connection that we honor today.

Love is perhaps the most profound experience we know on this earth and the union of two souls is cause to celebrate.

Today, N & N, we stand as witnesses to the promises you will offer to one another, as you express your intention to stand by each other and to build a future together.

May the love that has called you together grow ever brighter and brilliant with each sunrise, and may your promises offered today bring you joy and great delight in one another for all the days to come.

Here a reading or two may be offered

The Declarations

The minister asks:

N, will you take N to be your lifepartner? Will you stand by him/her no matter what happens, respecting him/her as a person, understanding his/her needs and enjoying his/her love for the rest of your life?

N: I will.

N, will you take N to be your lifepartner? Will you stand by him/her no matter what happens, respecting him/her as a person, understanding his/her needs and enjoying his/her love for the rest of your life?

N: I will.

The Promises
The couple turns and faces each other. They join hands and take turns saying:

Promise Option 1
N: From this moment, I, N, take you N as my best friend and partner for life. I promise to laugh with you in joy, support

you in the challenges and grow with you in love. I promise to be faithful to you alone and give you my unconditional love. With every beat of my heart I love you. This is my promise to you.

or

Promise Option 2
I, N, take you, N, as my partner for life.
I pledge to share my life openly with you,
to speak the truth to you in love.
I promise to honor and tenderly care for you,
to cherish and encourage your own fulfillment as an individual
for the rest of my life. This is my promise to you.

or the couple can write their own promises.

Exchange of Rings (if applicable)

The minister says:
These rings given and received are tokens of the covenant made this day between N&N this day. Let these rings say to all that your commitment is deep and life-long.

Each person repcats after the minister:

N: N, this ring is a token of my faithfulness and love, and a symbol that all I have I share with you.

The Final Blessing
The minister says:
N&N, your love has united you this day. May it continue to strengthen you and lead you forward on a journey of blessing

and happy adventures. May you continue to dream together, to hope together, and always follow your hearts.

May your lives together be joyful and content. May your love be bright as the stars and serve as a beacon for all. May your love be as warm as the sun, as wild as the oceans, and enduring as the mountains.

Conclusion

N&N, you have declared your love for each other and your hopes for the future. You have expressed your intention to live in a loving, committed relationship and have exchanged intentions and rings as tokens of your promises.

It is my pleasure to pronounce that you are united by Love as partners for life.

You may seal your promises with a kiss.

Copyright 2017 Bishop Deborah Vaughan
http://www.holyangelscommunity.com/
Used with permission

Renewal of Vows

A Vow Renewal can be as simple as you standing with the couple or as elaborate as the original wedding. Sometimes there has been a challenge in the marriage that prompts a couple to recommit to one another. More often it is a landmark anniversary that signals a celebration.

A Celebration of Love - *A Renewal of Vows*

N and N, today we celebrate the love that has brought you together, and the bond that has given you such joy and meaning since your original vows.

Even as Love has called you together, weaving your lives into one, we honour the journeys that have brought you to this point. We recognize the separate paths, memories, traditions, hopes and loves that have brought you through lessons and triumphs to this place of choice. Today, you choose each other again with a sacred and profound intention.

As you have learned, marriage is not intended to be a unity where differences cease to exist. Rather, it is a relationship where you can be fully and honestly yourself, sharing at the deepest level all that life is and all that you are. It is not always an easy road, but it is a place where Love flourishes at its deepest root.

As you renew your vows and your commitment to one another, may you be blessed, strengthened and affirmed in your journey and may the love you share continue to blossom and grow.

Optional Reading or other reading can be included here:

I'd Marry You Again

With tiny tears that glistened,
My eyes were fixed on you;
and thinking of the life we'd share,
we softly said, "I do."
Our hearts were knit together
from the time that we first met;
and memories were gathered
that we never will forget.

While daily living life with you,
you saw the real in me;
and still you chose acceptance,
a loving mystery.
With many happy times gone by,
and other when we cried;
some days we'd share so endlessly,
while other days we'd hide.
With all the ups and downs we've had
in learning to be friends;
I know that in this heart of mine
I'd marry you again.

The Declaration

N, will you take *N* to be your wife? Will you continue to stand by her no matter what happens, respecting her as a person, understanding her needs and enjoying her love from this day forth?
N: **I will.**

N, will you take *N* to be your husband? Will you stand by him no matter what happens, respecting him as a person,understanding his needs and enjoying his love from this day forth?

N: **I will.**

The Renewal of Vows –

Option 1
(The couple faces each other and repeats after the officiant)
N: In the light of our love and in thanksgiving for all our years together, I, *N*, take you, *N*, to be my wife/husband/lifepartner, to laugh with you in joy, to grieve with you in sorrow, to continue grow with you in love, to cherish you with my whole being, and to be faithful only to you.
I offer you my strength and support; I offer you my friendship. N, I offer you my love for as long as we both shall live.

Option 2
N: From this moment, I, **N**, continue to take you **N** as my husband/wife/lifepartner. I promise to love, honour, encourage, and support you through our life together. I promise to continue to stand by you and uplift you in mind and spirit, so that through our union, we can accomplish more than we would alone. This is my vow to you.

Option 3 – Traditional Vows:
With joy and gratitude, I reaffirm that I N, take you N, to be my husband/wife/lifepartner

To have and to hold from this day forward;
for better, for worse,

for richer, for poorer,
in sickness and in health,
to love and to cherish
for the rest of our lives.
This is my solemn vow.

Ring Ceremony

The rings are given to the officiant.
These rings given and received are tokens of the renewal of
the covenant made this day between **N&N**. Just as the circle
of the ring has no beginning and no end, so too their love is
unending. Just as the metal is pure and strong, so too the
bond between them is certain and steadfast. Let these rings
say to all that your commitment is deep and life-long.

N: N, this ring is a token of my faithfulness and love, and a
symbol that all I have I will always I share with you.

*Here a sand ceremony, Unity candle, rose petal ceremony or
other element can be included.*

The Blessing

As you have recommitted to one another in these sacred vows
as partners for life, remember that your bond together is
upheld and supported at all times by Love in whom we live
and move and have our being.

May you be blessed in your work and in your companionship,
in your sleeping and in your waking, in your joy and in your
challenges. May you be given all that you need to live out the
vows and the promises you have reaffirmed this day and may
harmony, serenity and blessing be the hallmark of your life
together.

Pronouncement

N and N, you have upheld your love for each other and your hopes for the future. You have renewed your solemn covenant with each other and have symbolized it by joining hands, renewing vows and exchanging rings.

I now pronounce that you have today reaffirmed your life commitment to one another and that are husband and wife (lifepartners, etc.)

Go forth in love and friendship and may you be blessed for the rest of the days of your lives.
You may seal your vows with a kiss.

Copyright 2017 Bishop Deborah Vaughan
http://www.holyangelscommunity.com/
Used with permission

Handfasting

Not everyone is comfortable doing a handfasting ceremony, but it is a very old tradition that goes back thousands of years. The act of tying ribbons around the wrists of the couple is a very visual symbol of their intention to unite in marriage. This ceremony is based on a more pagan celebration of marriage. You can change the wording as necessary.

The Gathering of the Community

We have come together today to celebrate the joining together of N&N. There are many things to say about marriage. Much wisdom concerning the joining together of two souls has come our way through all paths of belief, and from many cultures. With each union, more knowledge is gained and more wisdom gathered.

Marriage is a bond to be entered into only after considerable thought and reflection. As with any aspect of life, it has its cycles, its ups and its downs, its trials and its triumphs. With full understanding of this, N&N have come here today to be joined as one in marriage.

N&N, if either of you know a reason why the two of you may not be joined in marriage, you must declare it now.

The Hand Fast

the couple joins hands

May the words spoken on this day bind you.
May these ribbons tie you together for life.

May the God and Goddess bless these ribbons
and give your union strength.

the first ribbon is tied

Blessed be this union with the gifts of the East:
communication of the heart, mind, and body,
fresh beginnings with the rising of each Sun,
and the knowledge of the growth found in the
sharing of silences.

the second ribbon is tied

Blessed be this union with the gifts of the South:
warmth of hearth and home,
the heat of the heart's passion,
and the light created by both to illuminate the darkest of
times.

the third ribbon is tied

Blessed be this union with the gifts of the West:
the deep commitments of the lake,
the swift excitement of the river,
the refreshing cleansing of the rain,
and the all encompassing passion of the sea.

the fourth ribbon is tied

Blessed be this union with the gifts of the North:
firm foundation on which to build,
fertility of the fields to enrich your lives,
and a stable home to which you may always return.

The Betrothal

Do you N, take N to be your wife/husband/spouse/lifepartner, to be her/his constant friend, her/his partner in life, and her/his true love? To love her/him without reservation, honour and respect her/him, protect her/him from harm, comfort her/him in times of distress, and to grow with her/him in mind and spirit?
R: I do.

Do you N, take N to be your wife/husband/spouse/lifepartner, to be his/her constant friend, his/her partner in life, and his/her true love? To love him/her without reservation, honour and respect him/her, protect him/her from harm, comfort him/her in times of distress, and to grow with him/her in mind and spirit?
R: I do.

Now you are bound one to the other
With a tie not easy to break.
Take the time of binding
Before the final vows are made
To learn what you need to know -
To grow in wisdom and love.
That your marriage will be strong
That your love will last
In this life and beyond.

The Marriage Vows

N: Today, as I give myself to you. My mind is clear and my commitment is strong. I take you to be my wife. I will never leave you nor forsake you; I will spend all my days at your side. We will share a lifetime of eternal love.

N: Today, as I give myself to you. My mind is clear and my commitment is strong. I take you to be my husband. I will never leave you nor forsake you; I will spend all my days at your side. We will share a lifetime of eternal love.

Un-tying of the Ribbons

The Exchanging of the Rings

N: I give this ring as my gift to you. Wear it and think of me and know that I love you.

N: I give this ring as my gift to you. Wear it and think of me and know that I love you.

In the name of the God and Goddess, I now pronounce you husband and wife.

Signing of the Register

Blessing

May your mornings bring joy and your evenings bring peace.
May your troubles grow few as your blessings increase.
May the saddest day of your future
Be no worse than the happiest day of your past.
May your hands be forever clasped in friendship
And your hearts joined forever in love.
Your lives are very special,
God has touched you in many ways.

May his blessings rest upon you
And fill all your coming days.

Introduction of the Couple

Copyright 2017 Bishop Deborah Vaughan
http://www.holyangelscommunity.com/
Used with permission

Christian Version of Handfast

Needed: Three ribbons or cords, one of which is white. 1 Coloured ribbon/cord is to be passed around. 1is to be charged andheld by the couple prior to the ceremony. 1 is to represent the Trinity.

Ribbon or cord is passed around to the wedding guests at the beginning of the ceremony (determined by the size of the group) Each person holds it and infuses their best wishes and love into the ribbon as they hold it and then pass it to the next person who does the same.... **ribbons are placed on a table.**

Today we gather together with *N & N* to celebrate this transformational moment in their lives as they join hearts and hands in love to become one, together in marriage.

Your separate journeys have brought you to this intersecting place in time, a place of great happiness and fulfillment. You have found your heart's desire in one another. You have discovered that one person within whom you recognize love most completely. It is that beautiful connection that we honour today as you come to be married.

The marriage covenant is a mystical exchange of promise and intention that offers you both continued joy, affirmation, respect and support for the rest of your lives.

The promises you make today, these cherished words that speak of the deep and abiding love that you share, will see you through every storm and celebration to come.

Today *N & N* , by joining hands, exchanging vows and rings and expressing your intention to build a future together, your lives are transformed and now merge into one.

May the love that has called you together grow ever brighter and more brilliant with each sunrise, and may these vows offered today bring you joy and great delight in one another for all the days to come.

(If readings are to be incorporated, they are included here.)

The Declarations

N, will you take N to be your wife/lifepartner? Will you stand by her/him no matter what happens, respecting her/him as a person, understanding her/his needs and enjoying her/his love for the rest of your life? **N:** I will.

N, will you take N to be your husband/lifepartner? Will you stand by her/him no matter what happens, respecting her/him as a person, understanding her/his needs and enjoying her/his love for the rest of your life? **N:** I will.

The Vows *(The couple face each other and repeat after Deborah)*

Option 1

N: From this moment, I, N, take you N as my best friend for life. I promise to be your faithful partner and give you my unconditional love. I pledge to honour, encourage and support you through our walk together. I promise to work at our love and always make you a priority in my life. With every beat of my heart I will love you. This is my solemn vow.

Option 2

N: From this day forward, I, N, take you *N* as my best friend for life, the one I will live with, dream with, and love forever. I look with joy down the path of our tomorrows, knowing we will walk it together side by side, hand in hand, and heart to heart. Before us lies an open road, filled with adventure and love. I choose to spend today, and all of my tomorrows, with you as my friend, my wife/husband and my love. This is my solemn vow.

Option 3 - Traditional

I, N, take you, N, to be my wife/husband/lifepartner/spouse
To have and to hold from this day forward;
for better, for worse, for richer, for poorer,
in sickness and in health, to love and to cherish
for the rest of our lives.
This is my solemn vow.

Option 4

N: I, N, take you N, to be my wife/husband/lifepartner/spouse
To laugh with you in joy
To grieve with you in sorrow
To grow with you in love,
To be faithful to you alone for as long as we both shall live.
This is my vow to you.

Option 5

N: I, N, take you N, to be no other than yourself- loving what I know of you, trusting what I do not yet know, with respect for your integrity, and faith in your love for me, through all our years, and in all that life may bring us.

I promise to try to be ever open to you, and to do everything in my power to support you in becoming the person you are yet to be. I promise to love you, to respect you, to laugh with you and to soothe your tears.

I promise to share my life openly and honestly with you; to bring to you the best in me, and to dedicate my time and my energy to you, and to the unfolding of who we are becoming.

I promise to place our relationship at the heart of my life, and not to let the flurry of the everyday eclipse our sacred commitment to one another. This is my solemn vow.

Option 6 – Your own vows

The Handfast (Bride and Groom hold hands)

Priest takes the cords/ribbons from table.

Priest: N&N, you have made a covenant with each other to join your lives as a married couple before God and these witnesses. These ribbons/cords are a further symbol of your connection this day.

This first ribbon/cord represents your hopes and dreams as a couple together, energized by your love. (ties ribbon around both left wrists) As this ribbon/cord is tied, so are your lives now bound as one, spirits and intentions united through this sacrament of marriage.

As this second ribbon/cord is tied remember that you are surrounded by family and friends who love you. Within the very fibres of this fabric are infused all the hopes of your friends and family for your new life together. As we tie this knot, be affirmed by all their desires, dreams, love and happiness for you.

As this third ribbon/cord is tied, remember that you are always surrounded and supported by God, in whom we live and move and have our being. You are bound together in love and blessed by the Father and the Son and the Holy Spirit, who unites you in love this day.

Hands

Ring Ceremony

(The rings are given to the Officiant. The couple joins left hands and repeat after the Officiant)

These rings given and received are tokens of the covenant made this day between N & N. Just as the circle of the ring has no beginning and no end, so too their love is unending. Just as the metal is pure and strong, so too the bond between them is certain and steadfast. Let these rings say to all that your commitment is deep and life-long.

N: N, this ring is a token of my faithfulness and love, and a symbol that all I have I share with you.

N: N, this ring is a token of my faithfulness and love, and a symbol that all I have I share with you.

(ribbons are loosened and couple holds hands)

(If additional elements are to be included, they usually are included here.)

The Blessing

As you are joined together in these sacred vows as partners for life, remember that your bond together is upheld and supported at all times by Love in whom we live and move and have our being.

Now you will feel no rain for each of you will be shelter for the other. Now you will feel no cold for each of you will be warmth for the other. Now there is no loneliness for you, because though you are two persons there is only one life before you. As you now enter your life as married partners, may your days together be happy and long.

Pronouncement

N & N, you have declared your love for each other and your hopes for the future. You have made a solemn covenant with each other and have symbolized it by joining hands, by declaring your vows, and by exchanging rings. I now pronounce that you are now husband and wife/ lifepartners.

May your love continue to unite you so that you may be faithful to the vows that you have made this day, and may you live together in joy and peace till your lives end.

You may kiss the bride./You may seal your vows with a kiss.

Signing of the Register

Announce the Couple

Recessional

Appendix Three: Additional Elements for Your Ceremony

Please note that these Elements are my own composition and are under my copyright. You may use them because you have purchased this book. Please do not share this material with other officiants – instead, refer them to this book for purchase.

Unity Candle

There are several variations on this that work well.

Option 1 – The mothers of the couple come forward. The officiant lights the taper candles and offers them to the mothers, who then give the lit tapers to their son or daughter.

Option 2 – The officiant light the tapers and hands one to each of the couple.

Option 3 – The candle is lit <u>at the beginning</u> of the service as a memorial to those who passed on and cannot be present with the couple. Pictures of loved ones can be displayed beside the candle. The couple lights the one candle as a sign of their loving connection with those who've passed on and a symbol of their new life, united as one.

Ceremony
(The couple brings two taper candles, centre pillar candle and candle holders)

Officiant: As we celebrate N&N's marriage this day we offer a symbol of their commitment.

(Officiant lights two candles. If moms included they are now called forward. The couple each receives a lit candle)

If memorial is included:

Officiant: As we begin this celebration, the couple will light a special candle to signify their intention to become one in holy matrimony this day. And as love has brought them together, we also remember those loved ones who inspired and cared for them while in this life and we honour all who are in our hearts and minds on this beautiful day where love is celebrated.

As unity candle ceremony only:

Officiant: These candles represent your lives before today, lives with separate families, friends and paths. As you light the One candle, it is a sign that you are now joined as one, shining together as brightly as the love you share.

They light the one candle.

N and N, on this, your wedding day we celebrate your love. This flame represents the complete oneness of your lives, bound together by love, from this time forth and forevermore.

Copyright 2017 Bishop Deborah Vaughan
http://www.holyangelscommunity.com/
Used with permission

This is a beautiful ceremony that takes place after the ring exchange. It can be expanded to include children as well. If the parents exchange roses they may wish to offer another colour rose, gerberas, seasonal flowers or even a silk flower

The Rose Ceremony (couple brings roses, flowers and a vase)

Officiant: For centuries, a red rose has been the symbol of love that is deep, true and abiding. The red rose is the colour of fire and passion. It is bold, yet has a fragrance that is delicate and sweet. It is the perfect symbol for you to share as you begin your life together.

Officiant gives rose to first person.

1st person: "N, I give you this rose as a symbol of my love. May every day of our life be as beautiful and as perfect as this rose."

Officiant gives rose to 2nd person.

2nd person: "N, I give you this rose as a symbol of my love. May every day of our life be as beautiful and as perfect as this rose." (Roses are placed in a simple vase if ceremony ends here.)

If family are included they are now called forward

Officiant: These beautiful flowers symbolize the purity of your parents' love for each other and each of you. As you are called to be one family now, so you receive this, a token of your new relationship with each other bound in love.

The Couple gives each family member a flower and says:
"We love you forever and we hold you in our heart." (or
words to that effect)

Officiant: And as a sign of your commitment to be so joined by love, in this circle of N and N's beloved, please put your flowers in the vase.

(family return to seats)

Copyright 2017 Bishop Deborah Vaughan
http://www.holyangelscommunity.com/
Used with permission

The Wine Box Ceremony

Materials : two bottles wine, locking box, prewritten letters in sealed envelopes.

Note: I really don't use the exact text written below any longer, finding it rather negative on their happy day. The intention of this element is that the bride and groom write each other love letters and put a few bottles of wine into a box that can lock or be sealed, agreeing to open it later if the marriage runs into difficulties. I have also heard this referred to as the "First Fight Box."

Variations:

1.Invite your guests to write thoughts and best wishes during the reception, which will be locked into the box and read when it is opened again.

2.Every few years on your anniversary, open the box and read the notes. Have new ones ready to go into it. In this way you will get a picture of your life together over time.

3.Set up a date a year or two down the road to have the wedding party over for a party. Open the box, drink the wine, read the letters, watch the wedding video and reminisce.

General Text of ceremony:

N&N, I have asked you to find a strong box that will hold two bottles of wine (or drink of choice). In addition, I have asked each of you to write a letter to one another, expressing your thoughts about the good qualities that you have found in your future partner, as well as your reasons for falling in love with each other. Under no condition were you to read each other's letter, and that you were to seal them in individual envelopes and put them in the boxes with the wine.

Should you ever find your marriage encountering serious difficulties, I ask that before you make decisions that could affect your marriage together, that you both open the box, drink some wine together, and then venture off into separate rooms to read the letters that you wrote to one another when you were united as a couple.

By reading these love letters, you will reflect upon the reasons that you fell in love with each other in the first place. The hope here is that there will never be a reason for you to open this box, unless, of course, it is for your 25 year anniversary!

N&N, I now ask that you close the box and lock it.

Copyright 2017 Bishop Deborah Vaughan
http://www.holyangelscommunity.com/
Used with permission

The Sand Ceremony

This is becoming a very popular addition to wedding ceremonies. It can be a simple activity between the couple, or it can involve children, family members, friends... every wedding is different.

It is easiest to let the couple handle the purchase of a kit and colours of sand, especially if many people are involved. The more people, the larger the centre container should be.

For the couple, it is a visual symbol of their lives joining together in marriage. For a family it is a keepsake and reminder of the special day when they celebrated the wedding and they became family in a new way. As they see all the colours of sand in the container, it becomes a wonderful touchpoint to the special occasion.

For the Couple:
Sand Ceremony *(needed: two vials containing different colours of sand and a larger empty container with a stopper or lid.)*

Officiant: As a further expression of their love, N and N will share in this Sand Ceremony, a beautiful expression of Unity.

Formed over time from rock and wind and water, sand has been part of the life of the world for eons and speaks to us of steadfast witness to the passing years. The sands of time symbolize dedicated and lasting love, eternal and soulful, joyful and limitless.

As you pour your individual containers of sand into this glass vessel- which itself is created from sand, melted and shaped to create this vessel- the colours are joined together, mingling in a beautiful pattern as unique as your spirits together.

(The couple takes turns pouring their sand into the container until it is full)

Officiant: Repeat after me.
You are my love for eternity. I blend with you. My heart, like these grains of sands now merges with yours. I am yours. You are mine. We are together forever like the sand, like the wind. We are one.

Officiant: As we can see, the grains of sand can never be separated. The colours of both containers are clearly there, but can never be put back into the original vials. There is unity and yet, there are distinctive parts. This symbolizes your union – two souls now united as the one.

Appendix Four : For Ontario Officiants
The Mysteries of the Paperwork

Part of your responsibility as officiant is to ensure that the paperwork for the wedding is properly taken care of.

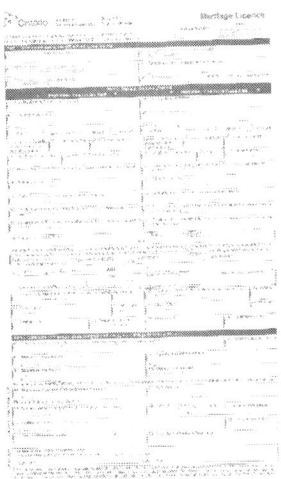

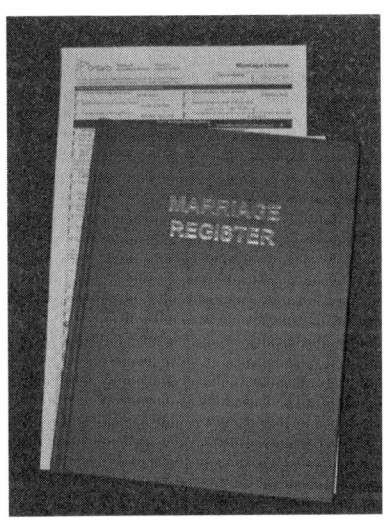

| Wedding Licence | Marriage Register (Blue Book) |

The Wedding Licence
(Which I think should be "license", but it spelled licence on the paperwork, so what the heck)

The Wedding licence is purchased by the couple. They are the only ones who can apply for it, although if both cannot be there, the other can apply, bringing along both sets of ID etc. There is a swearing in process involved stating that the information given is true.

Note that people who have been divorced outside Canada will NOT be able to apply for a marriage licence until they have their divorce papers verified by a Canadian lawyer and approved by the Registrar's Office in Thunder Bay. This can take up to 3 months.'

Once the marriage licence is obtained it is valid for 90-days.

We also have a **blue registration book** given to us by the province. This should be kept in a very safe place because is it a legal registry with details of the weddings we perform. Should the couple lose their certificate, we are called upon to supply the details for the government.

At the Wedding

For a wedding, you will need to bring your ceremony and your blue book with you. Upon arrival, ask for the couple's licence. It comes in two parts: a long form and a second sheet with a tear away section.

Find a place where you can write. Separate the second page, save the top of the form (I tuck it into the blue book) and fill in the half sheet that says "Record of Solemnization of Marriage. You'll note that it asks for the names of the couple, which you'll find in full on the long form. It asks for the date, the town/city and your name. There are also places for the two witness to sign later in the ceremony. It also has the licence number.

In the next empty page of your blue registration book, enter the name of the couple in the order they appear on the licence. So if the groom is on the left hand side, put his name in the book on the left hand side. You don't need to fill it out at the wedding, there often isn't time. Just place their names so that the blue book matches that of the wedding licence order.

I usually leave the register with the licence bookmarking the page on the table where they will be signing it.

The Signing of the Register

At the signing of the register, invite the bride to be seated. Open the blue book and take out the licence laying it on the free page. Have the bride sign on her side of the licence where it says "applicant" or "joint applicant" and then in the book on the corresponding side where it says "spouse." She signs her maiden name or the signature she used on the licence. Have the groom sign opposite her in the two places. Photographers often wish to take some shots at this point.

Next invite the witnesses over. They sign in three places: under the bride or groom in the licence and the blue book (they do not need to write their address but if there is time, invite them to do so) and also on the half sheet.

Now the half sheet is complete! Give this to the bride and groom as a record of the marriage. They keep this.

Following the Ceremony

Once you are home, it is time to fill in the rest of the paperwork. Everything on the long form needs to be transferred into the book. It isn't quite in the same order, so be alert.

Please use an ink pen to fill in the paperwork. Either blue or black ink is fine.

Completing the Marriage Register Step By Step:

In the blue book you'll see that it asks whether the wedding was by licence or banns. Tick licence.

Check the appropriate box for never married, widowed, or divorced for each person according to the licence.

Transfer the names of the couple into the blue book from lines 7 & 8, 24 & 25 in the licence. Last Name and First/Other Names

Record the Age and Date of Birth according to the licence.

Don't worry about "Occupation" unless you happen to know it.

Under the Religious Denomination category copy exactly what is stated in the Licence.

Residence: Record the address. If the couple are living together, just write "same" in the column for the other person.

Record the Father's Name, last name first.
Record the Mother's Name, Last name first.

The Signature section should be complete on both sets of documents.

The bottom part of the blue book register is our verification of the wedding.
 Record the Place of Marriage and the address.
 County, District or Regional Municipality: This will vary according to the venue
 Your Signature and the date of the wedding

Most Important:
The licence number - found on the top right corner of the licence in red.
The date of Issue: found in Part 1, line 1 of the licence at the top left.
The Place of Issue: Line 2 to the right of the date.

If you make a mistake in the book or the licence, put brackets around it and initial. There are instructions on the second half of the tear away that you keep for your records.
(Part 4, Form 2)

Completing the Marriage Licence:

Most of the licence has been filled in and recorded already. The bottom section, Part 3, is our responsibility.

Line 40 - Where was the wedding held (city, town, province) What municipality, region or county did it take place?
Line 41 - Date of the wedding
Line 46 - Your signature and the date of the wedding
Line 48 - Your printed name, last, first and middle
Line 49 - Status - check Clergy or if you are not ordained, under "other" write registered
        celebrant or whatever you were instructed to do in your training.
Line 50 - Your full address and 51- telephone number
Line 51 - Your registration number as given to you by the province
Line 52- Your organization or Church

Easy as that!

Put the completed licence into the manila envelope provided. Postage is already paid. I usually put some tape on the back for extra security.

As with all things, if you have any questions, do not hesitate to call the marriage hotline.

Appendix Five: Wedding Intake Sheet

Wedding Information Form
Your Name
Address
phone, email, website

Today's Date:

Have either been divorced outside of Canada? N___

Y___

Wedding____   Renewal of Vows____   Commitment
Ceremony____

Elopement _____   Do they have witnesses_____

Price quoted:

Payment received:
Balance owing:
Method of Payment:

Bride:
Address of Bride:

email:
phone:

Groom:
Address of Groom:

email:
phone:

Wedding Details:
Date of Wedding
Scheduled Start Time
Location:

Type of Ceremony:
Elopement ____   Short Civil___   Non-religious____
Spiritual____
Religious___   Mixed Faith ____   Other____

Wedding Party:
Number of Attendants: ___
Flower girl? _____
Ring Bearer? _____

Is the Bride being escorted? _____   By Whom?_____

Rehearsal needed?

Ceremony:

Memorial Candle?
Vow Option selected

Reading(s)?
Read by:

Special Elements:
Sand ceremony?   **For how many?**   **Sand colour choices**

Flower ceremony?

Wine box ceremony?

Unity Candle?

Other?

Music
DJ or special musical guest?
Bringing own songs?

NOTES:

Conclusion

Officiating at weddings can be a truly rewarding experience. Your part in the celebration will set the tone for the rest of the day. For those who get involved with their couples and participate fully in their joy and excitement, each wedding becomes more than "work" for us. Every blessing to you as you assist the families who call upon you.

The Savvy Celebrant

Do you have a question? Would you like to discuss an issue with someone who has been in your shoes? Deborah Vaughan is available for consultations and coaching. Visit www.thesavvycelebrant.com

Do you need a boost of confidence, would a course in a specific area assist you? Visit www.celebrantdevelopment.com for upcoming sessions.

23069308R00058

Printed in Poland
by Amazon Fulfillment
Poland Sp. z o.o., Wrocław